June, '87

To the Kielys —
        Hope these pictures will
stir some fond memories of Japan.
See you in Conn.!
                Sayonara,
                    The Haleys

The Japanese Inn
RYOKAN

The Japanese Inn
RYOKAN

A Gateway to Traditional Japan

Preface by Donald Richie

Shufunotomo Co., Ltd.
Tokyo, Japan

Concept & Art Direction: Yutaka Iwakiri
Text: Donald Richie, Sadao Miyamoto
Interviews: Keiko Aota, Yurie Horikoshi
Photographs: Toshiaki Sakuma

First printing, 1985

Published by Shufunotomo Co., Ltd.
2-9, Kanda Surugadai
Chiyoda-ku, Tokyo
101 Japan

Printed in Japan

ISBN4-07-974222-3

Preface

Travelling in Japan is one of the delights of being there. The country is not merely Tokyo, and outside the capital stretches a land which is in many ways more traditional. This the traveller should experience.

He should do so because the traditional, while perhaps no less authentic than the modern, has been around longer, it has achieved a kind of patina, it carries more meanings and it more rewards regard.

So, the first step toward a discovery of the traditional in Japan is to travel away from Tokyo, preferably to the smaller towns, or simply to well-situated villages. And once there do not stay at the station hotel, no matter its apparent convenience. Stay instead at the best *ryokan* in the place.

There are a number of reasons for doing so. One is that the food will invariably be good, another is that the rooms and bedding will be immaculate. But the real reason is that the Japanese inn remains traditional.

Everything is Japanese-style—everything important at any rate. Though there may nowadays be a television set or a baby refrigerator in the rooms, along with a telephone and an airconditioner, these relics of modernity are soon forgotten in an appreciation of the overwhelming Japaneseness of the experience.

One sits on *zabuton* cushions on the *tatami* and sleeps on the laid-out *futon*. One sips the fragrant *ocha,* drinks warmed saké, and eats a cuisine entirely Japanese. After, or before, one bathes in the soothing *ofuro* and, later, one strolls in a crisp *yukata* kimono.

All this is very Japanese indeed, but equally enjoyable is the feeling of tradition which one is also experiencing: the view of the garden and the consequent realization that one is not so separated from nature as one had thought; the fact that the very construction of the inn (raw woods, stones, all natural materials) as well as the construction of your meal (fresh local foods in season) insists upon a closeness with nature which we had almost forgotten existed.

Just as traditional is the observance that nature includes human nature. The service in the Japanese inn is of a degree not to be experienced anywhere else. It is such that you, become a grateful guest, and begin behaving as one. This means that the inn becomes your host, and a most gracious one it is. The resulting symbiosis perhaps also reflects a traditional Japanese ideal: man creates a harmony with nature, in so doing he also creates a harmony among his members.

One of the results of the *ryokan* experience is that one experiences a world, that of tradition, which has in some ways vanished and yet in others, as in the Japanese inn, still continues.

Any drawbacks? Not really—*futon* sleeping is good for you, so is the bath and the food. Perhaps having the maid around all of the time, bringing you this and that, sitting and serving you at meals, becomes a bit overpowering. But this is part of the traditional exprience. The only drawback really is that many big *ryokan* no longer offer this tradition. They have coke machines in the game room—that sort of thing. But if you choose the best in town, the one with the fine view, the famous one, then your time in the Japanese *ryokan* will be both enjoyable and rewarding. For here the past is present and tradition lives.

Donald Richie

Table of

Contents

The Ryokan and Traditional Culture

During the past century of vast social change in Japan the traditional has been gradually eroded. From Japan's emergence from isolation to its present mood of international economic expansion, the traditional civilization of the country has been slowly disappearing. Since Japan chose modernization and accepted Westernization there has been little motivation to retain the old, the traditional.

Yet, so much has in some way remained. The Japanese cuisine is more or less traditional. The Japanese architectural style has been incorporated, in some cases almost unchanged, into modern buildings. Even the clothing style of a once kimonoed populace is seen in the new Japanese fashions.

At the same time, much has been retained and formalized. This is true of the classical stage arts of Noh and Kyogen, of the later Kabuki as well. It is certainly true of the Japanese dance, of *ikebana* flower arranging, of the tea ceremony, and of many crafts: pottery, weaving, lacquer, etc.

Still, the visitor coming to Japan may well be forgiven for inquiring if the traditional exists at all other than in ceremonial situations. And one answer might be that, yes, in many places tradition is still very much alive—and among these is the Japanese *ryokan*.

In a proper *ryokan* one is greeted in the traditional manner, a deep bow from *tatami* matting of the traditional *genkan* entryway, and one is bade fare well in the same sincere and friendly fashion. During one's stay the attention one is given, the services rendered, are those of old-fashioned traditional hospitality—one centuries away from the perhaps cool dispatch of the Western hotel.

One of the attributes of the traditional in Japan is that nature be included. And it is in the *ryokan*. Not only in the natural woods of the building but also in the views of the garden and the surrounding natural beauty of the landscape. And not only in the perfect flower arrangement in the *tokonoma* alcove of the room but also in the food one is served in that room.

Tsuboniwa garden at the Tawara-ya.

Ryokan cuisine has *shun,* that word which connotes the flavor of the seasons. Seasonal food, locally bought and naturally prepared—this is the fare of the Japanese inn and here too, of course, it is the natural attributes which are most prized.

The Japanese inn also has that natural regard for nature which includes human nature as well. The way in which the women who serve you (formerly called *jochū-san*) react to your every wish, indicated or not, and the way in which the woman in charge (the *okami-san,* who may also be the owner to the inn) seeks to make your stay not only pleasant, but perfect—these ways are those of old Japan where a guest was to be honored.

So too the attentions of the *banto-san* and his assistants, the men who see you in and out of doors, who take care of your shoes and provide the umbrella if it rains. And those in the kitchen, the *itamae-san* who select the provisions and cook the meals, attending to the smallest of details and ensuring excellence.

It is said that such extraordinary service has now all but disappeared—particularly in the large inns of celebrated scenic sights or those of hot springs resorts. This may well be true. The very volume of people would preclude such private attention.

Yet traditional inns—where the building, the rooms, the food and the service are all traditional—still exist and some of these are indicated at the end of this volume.

So, in answer to the question as to whether tradition exists at all in this modern and Western-looking country, the answer must be: Yes, go to a *ryokan* and find it. For it is in the Japanese inn that one may discover or rediscover many of the finest traditions of Japan's traditional culture.

Above, the *genkan* entrance with its relaxing atmosphere welcomes the travelers at the Hiiragi-ya; *below,* a gate at the Asada-ya.

HISTORY

It is said that the first inn in Japan was built as early as the eighth century. Constructed by a monk named Gyoki, it was presumably a place at which travelling priests might stay. Certainly, inns for the laity were a later affair. These did not appear until the late Edo period, around the end of the eighteenth century. The reason was that it was only then that commercial trade within the country had increased to the point of inns being necessary. After the major roads were built, inns began to appear along them, the main customers being travelling merchants, pilgrims, the military and the clergy. Towns built around well-known temples and shrines, *monzen-machi,* usually had more than their share of inns as did the *onsen-machi,* spa towns, with their various attractions, medicinal and otherwise.

VARIETIES OF INN

There are many types of Japanese inns at present, categorized usually according to place and to use. A few are: those overlooking scenic beauty, celebrated or otherwise; those utilizing a hot spring; those with a large Japanese-style garden; those which used to be private villas; those noted for their food, the so-called *ryori-ryokan*; and those which simply preserve a long tradition.

At present there are some eighty thousand inns in Japan. Their tradition is quite different from the Japanese hotel, a Western importation. At the inn one is personally served by maids, one dines in one's room, one is served tea, and is in all ways treated much more as a guest than a customer. In return the customer is expected to behave as a guest. The anonymous rowdiness sometimes encountered among hotel guests is almost never seen at the Japanese inn. Clad in their light *yukata,* their good behaviour and the hospitality extended by the staff create the prized and cherished *ryokan* atmosphere, encountered in all such inns, no matter where in Japan they are located.

Top, front view of the Hiiragi-ya ; *upper middle,* the typical entrance of a garden *ryokan*—the Sanyo-so; *lower middle,* entrance of the Yagyu-no-sho the interiors of which show the influence of the *kendo* fencing; *bottom,* the Izu Nagaoka Sekitei the garden of which is constructed with hundreds of stones.

THE JAPANESE INN

Surrounded by trees or stands of bamboo, or by the quiet alleys of an old city, the Japanese inn is built to harmonize with its surroundings. In this it differs not only with its counterpart, the hotel, but also with Western-style structures in general. One might say that Western architecture seeks to challenge nature, to assert itself. Japanese traditional architecture, on the other hand, seeks to harmonize itself with nature, to suggest that it, though manmade, is also natural. One of the signs of this is the natural asymmetry of Japanese architecture. It is not that the traditional structure, the inn for example, is unbalanced but that the balance is not Western. Rather, it is the flexible and asymetric structural balance found in natural things. Wood constructure allows a flexibility that brick and stone do not. A new room, a new corridor, a new wing grow as naturally from the *ryokan* as does a new branch from the limb of a tree.

THE LOBBY

The most important thing to know about the *ryokan* lobby is that, originally, there wasn't any. The lobby you now find is a modern innovation, taken from the hotel. It has been constructed solely for convenience—a space for meeting visitors, for waiting while rooms are being prepared. Ordinarily you will be guided by the *roykan* maid directly from the entryway to your room with no more than a passing glance at the lobby.

THE GATE

All traditional *ryokan,* like all traditional Japanese homes, have gates. It is at once a barrier and a boundary. Signalizing the act entering, it emphasizes change. Passing through it one is in a different, private world. Often rocks create a small landscape and frame the entryway. The *ryokan* thus presents itself to its guest, showing itself at its best. At the same time, it welcomes.

THE ENTRYWAY

The entryway or, most often, entry "room" of the Japanese inn is called the *genkan*. The term itself comes from Zen Buddhist parlance and it means "the gateway to the esoteric path," as befits the entrance to a temple. Here is the dividing line between inside and outside and here one of the actions acknowledging this is the removal of the shoes. These will be polished and stored, to again reappear whenever you wish to go out. Here also kneel the welcoming *okami-*

san, the mistress, and her maids, when you first appear. This spare platform, often decorated by a screen or a large piece of ceramic, is the space from which the inner rooms are reached. It is one's introduction to the inn itself.

Opposite page: the lobby of the Yagyu-no-sho which combines Western styles with Japanese architecture; *bottom,* Japanese antique *hibachi* brazier. *Top,* Japanese *byobu* screen; *left,* gate at the Awata-sanso; *right above,* the entry at the Hiiragi-ya; *right below,* the entry at the Horai.

Above, a guest room at the Hiiragi-ya. *Left,* sliding reed doors; *center, shoji* corridor window; *right,* woven bamboo strip door.

THE ROOMS

Traditional Japanese-style rooms are best described as simple, but this simplicity is of a functional kind. One of the reasons for the atmosphere of Japanese room is that almost everything in it is intended for use. Just as the principles of Japanese traditional architecture show their function through their form—all structural supports visible, nothing hidden—so the furnishings of the room proclaim their use and nothing is pretending to be anything else.

The *tatami* floor mats, the *shoji* and *fusuma* sliding doors, even the wooden veranda doors, the *amado,* are all modular—the same size regardless the room. In fact the Japanese way of indicating room size is through reference to its number of *tatami* mats.

These comprise the basic permanent room. Added to this (and taken away as well) is the furniture. There is the low lacquered table, the *zabuton* cushions to sit on. These, however, are moved away when the bedding, the *futon,* is taken from its closet and laid out. Thus this basic room is living room, dining room and bed room all in one.

This functional simplicity continues. Just as the *tokonoma* is a decoration which is also a structural part, so even the decorated door transoms, the *ranma,* though beautiful in themselves also have their structural function—they let in light and they allow ventilation.

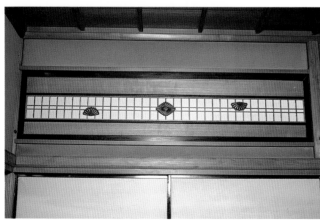

Left, door transom at the Sanyo-so; *center and right,* decorative door pulls. *Next page:* a guest room at the Tawara-ya.

THE TOKONOMA

The *tokonoma* is that alcove-like space found in traditional Japanese rooms where the *ikebana* floral decoration is arranged and where the hanging scroll is displayed. In the teahouse the arrangement is often simply made, of common flowers. But in more formal rooms the *ikebana* is often elaborate and along with the flowers and scroll fine antiques are often also displayed. Always, however, the *tokonoma* is thought of as a small stage which reflects the seasons—for these are the themes of both flower arrangements and scrolls.

Top: tokonoma alcoves at the Tsubaki; at the Sanyo-so; and at the Nara-ya. *Bottom,* tokonoma at the Sanyo-so.

Top left: view of the garden from the teahouse at the Awata-sanso; *top right,* inside the tearoom at the Arai Ryokan. *Bottom: matcha* green tea with Japanese sweet; entrance to the tearoom at the Torikyo; view of the teahouse at the Arai Ryokan.

TEA

When you have been taken to your room in a Japanese inn, the maid then reappears with green tea. This is either simple *ocha* steeped in its pot, or the whipped powdered *matcha* used in the tea ceremony. In either event it is accompanied by a small Japanese sweet. This traditional offering harks back, as do so many things about the *ryokan,* to the tea ceremony. Ritual though it is, it is friendship and hospitality that animate the art of tea. This and the closeness to nature symbolized by the natural simplicity of the tea utensils, the floral *ikebana* in the *tokonoma,* the very construction of the teahouse itself. Though the cup of tea brought you by your maid is a casual and friendly custom, it echoes the formal consideration of the tea-master. And the confection served with the tea also recalls *cha-no-yu,* the art of tea, in that it is a locally made sweet, and one which reflects the current season.

THE VIEW

The view from the room is one of the great pleasures of staying at the *ryokan*. Unlike the hotel, the Japanese inn is dedicated to an appreciation of nature and, consequently, a gratification of the senses. Just as the traditional *ryokan* seeks to blend with its surroundings, so these surroundings become the natural enclosure one views from one's room.

Thus, one's room is the traditional place for viewing. While it is possible to walk along the *nure-en*, open veranda, or—wearing the wooden clog-like *geta*—to wander in the garden itself, it is preferable, more fitting, to simply sit and enjoy the view.

Center, view of the garden form a guest room at the Tawaraya. *Above,* a second-floor guest room at the Arai Ryokan; *below,* iris in the garden; *right,* the garden with a small waterfall.

This view may be of the surrounding landscape but, more often, it is of the traditional garden, carefully laid out so that a different aspect is to be viewed from each room. Here in the autumn one may see a single tinted leaf floating in the *chozubachi* water basin. Or, in the winter, amid the black and the white, the red of single camellia bud.

Here too the sounds of nature: the songs of the birds in the early morning, the sighing of the wind passing through the nearby grove, or all night long the sound of the sea.

Left, a *karesansui* dry landscape garden; *above,* view of the garden from a guest room at the Kaika-tei; *below,* bamboo fence and stone lantern.

CORRIDORS

In traditional Japanese architecture corridors are not designed merely to connect rooms. Rather, they are considered a part of the living area and great care is given to their construction and to their appearance. Often, for example, a side wall will be left off so that a view of the garden is possible. Often too the corridor will consist merely of a roof, in case it rains, the "sides" being views of *ryokan* and its greenery. Sometimes as well the corridor walls will be decorated with rocks, plants, and lanterns, and with latticed papercovered windows which cast a soft and pearl-like light. Since corridors are not merely to connect, they often in the Japanese inn take on a life of their own, twisting and turning like a maze, their convolutions caused by the many wings and extra rooms which have been added to the old *ryokan*. All guest rooms thus come equipped with a map of the building so you can find where you are and not get lost.

STAIRS

In old Japan the only dwellings grand enough to need staircases were temples and palaces. Thus when homes and inns grew to two or more storeys, the staircase retained something of its sacerdotal character. There is consequently something decidedly ceremonial about the traditional Japanese staircase as seen in old Japanese inns.

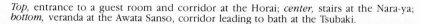
Top, entrance to a guest room and corridor at the Horai; *center,* stairs at the Nara-ya; *bottom,* veranda at the Awata Sanso, corridor leading to bath at the Tsubaki.

THE VERANDA

In traditional Japanese architecture the veranda, called *engawa,* a part of the room itself. These face often directly onto the garden. It is also a pleasantly neutral area: a part of the house yet also almost a part of the nature outside. Here one may sit and observe. Rain and snow stop here. One is shielded from the sun. Here one views the garden—almost oneself a part of it.

THE EAVES

Traditionally, the eaves of the Japanese rooms, called *hisashi,* are to the roof and ceiling as the *engawa* is to the floor. Here one is shielded from nature and yet still a part of it. One sits framed, protected and regards the garden.

Top, veranda at the Torikyo; *center,* patio corridor at the Tsubaki *bottom* annex corridor by pond at the Taikan-so, corridor built over the river at the Arai Ryokan.

LIGHTING

The ideal lighting for the Japanese room is natural lighting, particularly the soft and pearly light coming through the closed paper *shoji,* or the half-light from the corridor coming through the *ranma* transom. Candles and oil lamps used to serve for illumination and this effect is still prized in the age of electricity. The *andon,* a paper-paneled light-stand, now contains a lamp bulb instead of an oil lamp or a candle, but the effect is much as it was—a warm, soft glow shining through the Japanese paper and contrasting with the wood or bamboo frame of the lamp itself.

The quality of Japanese light depends much upon shadow. As Japan's great novelist, Junichiro Tanizaki, wrote in his well-known essay, *In Praise of Shadows:* "The beauty of a Japanese room depends on variations of shadows, heavy shadows against light shadows it has nothing else. Westerners are amazed at the simplicity of Japanese rooms, perceiving in them no more than ashen walls...Their reaction is understandable, but it betrays a failure to comprehend the mystery of shadows."

Opposite page: top, full view of the Tawara-ya *ryokan* at sunset; *below,* Tawara-ya guest room a night. *Above,* various types of Japanese lighting fixtures.

THE GARDEN

Japanese-style gardens, an indispensable part of the *ryokan* itself, are constructed in many sizes, shapes and varieties. No matter their differences, however, there is a common concept. Rocks, shrubs, plants, trees are all arranged as they would be in nature—the difference is that a balance has been achieved, a harmony imposed.

Though the Japanese love for nature has often been commented upon, it has rarely been examined. What it consists of is a very strong regard for what man can make of nature as it is. The wilderness is not admired but the naturalness of the man-made is. Indeed, until nature has been transformed by the hand of man—Japanese man—it is not considered natural at all. The Japanese garden is one of the results.

Top, the lawn at the Sanyo-so and a section of the buildings; *center,* the garden at the Hiiragi-ya; *bottom,* a stone pathway through iris at the Sanyo-so.

There are spacious gardens in which one may wander, as in a landscape, smaller versions of the large tour-gardens. There are the dry gardens, the *karesansui,* made of only sand and stones, the abstraction of a garden but containing the balance of harmonized nature. There are also the small gardens one associates with the tea-ceremony. All of these are different and yet the same in the they represent nature.

Built inside the building, surrounded by rooms and corridors there are also often *tsuboniwa,* very small gardens containing rocks, or a stone waterbasin, often covered with moss. These use the precious space by bringing nature inside. They share something with the concept of *shakkei,* borrowed scenery. Here nature has been borrowed and brought in. More properly the concept is seen in the main garden where, sometimes, a distant stand of trees or the flank of a mountain is so present that, in the context, it becomes a part of the garden itself.

Top, stepping stones at the Hiiragi-ya; *center,* a stepping stone pathway at the Taikan-so; *bottom,* a section of the buildings and the garden in early summer at the Kaika-tei.

ROCKS

Rocks, not often used as such in the Western garden, are most important to the Japanese garden. They are, it is said, the "bones" of the garden. They bring with them not only the feeling of distant, secluded nature, and their own natural beauty. They bring also a new dimension: time. Their history is weathered into their shape and color. Another use for rocks and stones which is both spatial and temporal occurs when they are arranged as steps. The stepping-stones are so arranged that the walk is guided and the tempo modulated. The pace must, given the placement and surface of these stones, be leisurely. One cannot rush through a Japanese garden. One must stroll, savor.

TREES

Trees and shrubs in the garden serve as outside walls. They seclude the building and at the same time they bring nature near. One of the ways of insuring this national proximety is to plant those things which change with the season—the *sakura* cherry-blossom, the maple leaf, these announce the spring and the autumn. When one looks at a *ryokan* it appears amid a sea of green. And when one looks from it there again are the shrubs, bushes, trees of green nature.

LANTERNS AND BASINS

The stone lanterns and stone water basins which decorate the traditional Japanese garden had their origins as practical adjuncts of the tea ceremony. The lanterns were a source of light and the *tsukubai* basins were used for the ritual rinsings before partaking of the tea ceremony itself. They became decorations in other than tea ceremony gardens only after garden and architecture rules were everywhere accepted at the end of the sixteenth century. These were work mainly of one man, the tea-master Sen-no Rikyu. It was his vision of a union of man and nature through rules which respected the both which accounts even now for this peaceful coexistence. It is still seen in Japan—in particular in its *ryokan*.

Top, stepping stones at the Arai Ryokan; bamboo garden gate at the Nara-ya; garden stones after the rain at the Hiiragi-ya. *Center,* stone bridge at the Hiiragi-ya, view of lotus ponds. *Bottom,* path in the garden of the Taikan-so; stone bridge at the Sanyo-so. *Right,* stone lantern and *tsukubai* at the Atami Sekitei.

RYOKAN FOOD

It is said that many aspects of Japanese culture are derived from the contrast of Japan's strongly defined seasons. If this is so, the traditional Japanese cuisine is certainly among these aspects. Fish, vegetables, fruit—what is in season is always welcomed and the first food of the season—the first *ayu* summer trout, the first of autumn's persimons, the first of winter's *mikan* oranges—are always looked forward to with pleasure.

Above, a summer beverage of matcha *green tea* and sake; summer dessert, watermelon, both as served at the Tsubaki. Below, summer *kaiseki* at the Hiiragi-ya.

Freshness is consequently a major consideration. Everything used must be palpably fresh. It must feel, taste, look fresh. This is one of the qualities of the Japanese cuisine. It appeals to the eye as well as to the sense of taste, and its textural quality is almost equally important. This freshness is observed in every step of the preparation. Fresh food lightly cooked with nothing additional added, seasonal dishes served for their own excellence. In addition, the traditional chef is concerned with the temperatures of the various foods. In the summer he serves mostly cold food with some hot; in the winter, mostly hot with some cold. There is, perhaps consequently, a rule that the food must be eaten within ten minutes after it has been dished out. In the finest *ryokan* your food is brought to you within this time allowance. Freshness and goodness is assured.

DINNER IN YOUR ROOM

The maid brings your dinner to your room. You do not order, except to indicate the time you prefer. The menu of the day has been decided and executed with care.

It will be comprised of a full number of dishes: *sashimi,* perhaps some shellfish, probably *tofu,* seasonal and regional specilities, and rice, tea and fruit.

You will also have indicated, however, what it is you prefer to drink with your meal. Since saké is to Japanese food as wine is to, say, French food, it is best to order a *choshi* bottle of the local saké warmed and brought in with you food.

In the finest inns the maid, your own personal one in that she has charge of your room as well as several others on your floor, serves you as you eat. She pours your saké and, when you are ready for it, she serves you the rice and later pours the green tea which ends every meal.

AFTER DINNER

Once the meal is completed in the Japanese inn it is nearly bedtime. So you can talk a short nocturnal walk in garden or can take another bath. When you return you will find that your maid has already laid out the *futon* and turned on the reading light.

Japanese *futon,* laid directly over the *tatami* matting, are surprisingly comfortable and much better for the body than most mattresses are. When the heavy quilt-like top *futon* is pulled up, one is quite ready for sleep.

If you decide to walk outside the inn make certain to inquire what time it closes its doors. *Ryokan* are very conservative. Most close at ten in the evening. In any event you will already have told your maid what time you wish to have breakfast and whether you want it Japanese-style or, something all inns can now make, Western.

Summer *kaiseki* at the Ryuguden.

Left, fresh seafood, the beginning of a *kaiseki* meal at the Tsubaki—the sake set is in the latticed box decorated with the seasonal wisteria. *Above,* the sake set laid out with appetizers at the Yagyu-no-sho; *below,* prepared mountain vegetables and seasoned rice at the Taikan-so.

BREAKFAST

When you return from your morning bath the *futon* have all been returned to the closet and the breakfast awaits.

The Japanese breakfast consists of *miso* soybean-paste soup, various kinds of *tofu* dishes, *nori* seaweed to be eaten with rice, *umeboshi* plums, and boiled fish—but there are many variations.

The Japanese breakfast can seem something of a challenge to those conditioned to coffee and toast but many claim that this first meal is one of Japan's most typical.

If you are staying for several days at the inn you should also know that lunch is never served. You many eat out, or the ryokan will make you a *bento* box lunch. Also, the *ryokan* keeps its own hours in meal-serving times as well. The time for eating breakfast is between seven and nine, usually, and guests are expected to accommodate themselves to this schedule. Also the evening meal is usually served only between six and eight. Obviously some exceptions are made when necessary but the *ryokan* is more a home than a hotel and the guest is expected to conform.

Opposite page: top, sesame *tofu, suimono* soup at the Tsubaki; *bottom:* rice gruel *okayu* at the Asada-ya. *Above, bento* lunch box at the Awata -sanso. *Below, tofu* served with scallions and spices at the Tawara-ya.

The entrance to the bath with its traditional *noren* curtain.

THE BATH

One of the joys of the Japanese inn is its *ofuro,* the bath. Depending upon the size and nature of the *ryokan* it comes in various sizes from the very large to the fairly intimate. Many inns now have small private baths just off the guest-room but it is still common for those at the *ryokan* to use the main bath.

Thus the baths themselves range from the smaller wooden baths to the large baths made of marble or rocks and stones. The wooden baths are constructed of fragrant white cedar or cypress. And the stools to sit on and pails used for rinsing are often of the same wood.

One of the particular joys of bathing occurs in the *onsen ryokan,* the hot-spring inn. Here the main bath is often large indeed, more like a pool than a tub. Often there is an

Bellow left, top, a *rotemburo* open-air bath at the Atami Sekitei; *bottom ,* a typical marble *ryokan* bath at the Nara-ya. *Below right,* wooden frame-roof using no nails at the Horai.

open-air hot bath as well, called a *rotemburo,* where one can bathe amid nature even in snow-covered winter.

Since the inn bath is often communial a certain etiquette is involved in its use. Going there one may, indeed should, wear the cotton *yukata* kimono supplied in your room. Since the entire ryokan is considered to be private space one is free to walk the corridors in what is actually a nightgown, something which is, of course, not tolerated in the public-space Western-style hotel. Once in the bathroom one washes before entering the water. Japanese tubs are used only for soaking—and only after one is clean. This means that many may enjoy the hot water. One should certainly get no soap in it and should, just as certainly, never unplug this communial bath once you have used it.

Above left, pail and stool used in the Japanese bath; *right,* the dressing room at the Horai. *Below left,* bath made of white cedar at the Nara-ya: below *right, top,* an open-air bath at the Izu Nagaoka Sekitei; *bottom,* a bath with a garden view at the Yagyu-no-sho.

SLEEPING IN FUTON

After dinner most guests leave their rooms to walk around the town or stroll about the garden. They wear their *ryokan* kimono-like *yukata*—though, unlike the kimono, the *yukata* is for both men and women worn with the left side over the right. If it is cold they put on their coat-like *tanzen* and may even wear *tabi* socks with their *geta* sandals. The stroll is to see the sights but it is also to give the maid the opportunity of clearing away the dinner dishes and the table on which the meal was served, and putting down the bedding.

This is called *futon.* It consists of a Japanese-style mattress placed directly on the *tatami,* a pair of sheets, and a big fluffy Japanese-style quilt. There is also a pillow, often also Japanese-style, firm, filled with rice husks. Each *futon* is single and for each guest a separate *futon* is prepared.

Returning from the walk—returning well before the *ryokan* is closed up for the night—the guest finds that his dining room has become an immaculate bedroom and that it is time for sleep.

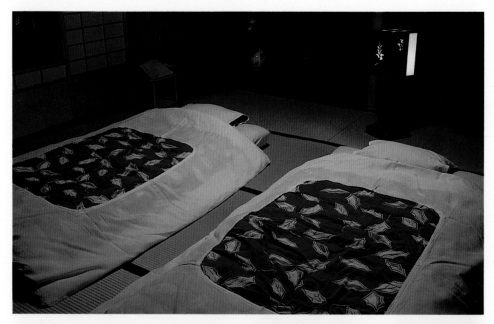

Above, guest room with *futon* at the Hiiragi-ya; *below,* a pair of *yukata* and *tanzen* at the Ryuguden ; a writing table at the Hiiragi-ya.

Some Typical Ryokan

TAWARA-YA

Located in the middle of Kyoto, the Tawara-ya is now world-famous—one of the most prestigious of all Japanese inns. During its three-hundred year history it has been for eleven generations managed by the same family. Here the traditional spirit of Japanese inn-keeping has been passed from one generation to another.

While committed to preserving this old tradition, the Tawara-ya is also open to innovations which may make the guest more comfortable—if this does not, of course, interfere with tradition. Thus such modern conveniences as air-conditioning and television have been unobtrusively installed in the guest rooms.

At the same time that television has made its discrete appearance care is taken that all of the traditional aspects remain. One of these is the small but famous *tsuboniwa,* the Japanese-style indoor garden which is so much a part of all *ryokan* and of the Tawara-ya in particular.

Opposite page: the *genkan* entryway. *Below, left,* view of a guest room from the garden; *right,* the veranda from the garden. *Bottom,* a typical meal made from seasonal foods.

SANYO-SO

The Sanyo-so is located at Izu-Nagaoka in the northern part of the Izu peninsula. Originally constructed as a villa for an old and wealthy family, it was remodeled and converted into an inn in 1947.

Its traditional buildings (it is in the restrained *sukiya* style) and its splendid garden were designed and built by the finest of architects and landscape gardeners, using generous amounts of time and money. Indeed, the impeccable structural proportions of the main building has made it widely known as a masterpiece of modern Japanese architecture.

The four-acre garden is scrupulously maintained by experienced gardeners. Its elegant atmosphere is enhanced by the iris pond, the open-air bath, the arbor, the teahouses and such rare artifacts as the stone lanterns from eighth-century China.

All of the twenty guest rooms face this splendid garden and the range of the Hakone mountains seen behind it. This changing natural panorama is reflected in the guest rooms, redecorated every season to match the different atmospheres of spring, summer, autumn and winter.

Left, a view of the Sanyo-so from the garden. *Opposite page:* the garden and grounds. *Below,* a typical summer meal. *Right, top,* view from a guest room; *center,* one of the larger guest rooms; *bottom,* the bath.

TSUBAKI

Located in Yugawara, a well-known hot-springs resort not too far from Tokyo, the Tsubaki is a *sukiya*-style inn surrounded by mountains, fresh air and the sound of streams. *Tsubaki* means "camellia" and the guest rooms are named after the different varieties of this flower.

An interesting feature of this *ryokan* is that every room comes with a garden view. Those on the first floor overlook the main garden. Those on the second floor, since the inn is built on a slope, have their own small gardens attached to their rooms.

The cuisine at the Tsubaki is Kyoto-style with seasonal delicacies served on the best lacquer and chinaware. These trays and dishes, designed or selected by the inn, are traditionally shaped to compliment the foods that they hold. It is care such as this which has made the Tsubaki, despite its relatively short history, one of the more distinguished inns.

Opposite page: a view of the garden from one of the guest rooms. *Above left,* a view of the Tsubaki in autumn; *above right,* the *izutsu* where water is drawn to fill the pond. *Below:* a view of the buildings housing the baths; a typical summer *kaiseki* meal; the *ryokan* at dusk; a room prepared for guests.

RYUGUDEN

Situated overlooking the lake Ashinoko, the Ryuguden is famous for its architecture which is modeled after that of the Byodo-in in Uji, itself one of the finest examples of early Japanese architecture.

Built in 1936, the building was originally at Lake Hamana but was moved to its present location in 1956. It has since these times been regarded as an architectural wonder, one which with its elaborate *shoin* style, its use of zelkova and white cedar throughout, would be impossible now to duplicate.

The luxuriousness of the Ryuguden is indicated by the fact that in its eight-acre space there are only twenty rooms and that each of these has a breathtaking view of Ashinoko and Mount Fuji beyond.

Opposite page: above, a view of the Ryuguden; *below,* a view of the lake with Mt. Fuji in the background; one of the guest rooms. *Left,* main hallway with chandelier; *right,* summer *kaiseki* with wisteria; *bottom,* the bath.

HORAI

Near the city of Atami, in Izusan, the Horai is famous for its hot spring baths and the six-acre garden which is carefully designed to harmonize with the view in the background: Sagami Bay, the mountain range of the Izu Peninsula and the silhouettes of the Izu islands in the distance— a view which is enjoyed from every guest room.

The Horai dates back to 1849 when the original villa, belonging to a viscount, was converted into an inn. The present building, remodeled in 1978, is in the authentic *sukiya* style.

The local hot springs are among the three oldest in Japan. There are some medical benefits particularly for those suffering from rheumatism and bronchitis and the main bath is considered one of the finest in the vicinity.

These amenities, plus the famous cuisine, and seasonal foods all from local sources, have helped to make this inn famous.

Right, the bath; *below,* the patio corridor.

Left, entrance, sea-food from Sagami Bay; *right,* the loppy; *below,* a guest room in traditional *sukiya* architectual style.

ASADA-YA

This old and famous inn was established in 1867 and its owner is the fifth generation of the family which has run this *ryokan*.

Located in Kanazawa, which because of the largely unspoiled beauty of its architecture is sometimes called the Kyoto of the Hokuriku district, near the Japan Sea. The inn well reflects the refined tastes of the Japanese tradition.

When the old building was rebuilt all of the concrete reinforcing was covered with fine wood. Thus was kept the appearance of age and elegance. At the same time the number of guest rooms were reduced. This is certainly a welcome anomaly in today's world where all things, including *ryokan,* are relentlessly enlarged. The old Asada-ya has thirty-three rooms. Now it has just five.

This means that the maximum number of guests which can be accommodated at one time

Above, view of the Asada-ya at dusk; *below, left,* the lobby with its traditional sunken "fireplace"; *top,* lobby with traditional doll-shelf for the March 3rd Girls' Day; *bottom,* guest room with interior garden.

are only twenty—five parties of four each. And, as this would indicate, the service extended to each guest is such that the name of Asada-ya is famous all over Japan.

Here the prevailing attitude is that the customer is a guest. The *okami-san* housekeeper strongly feels that the relationship is that of a host to those who come to visit and it is this belief that she also teaches the *jochu-san* maids.

The maids themselves are all adept in the traditional Japanese arts. All, for example, are sent out for lessons in the tea ceremony. They are also knowlegeable concerning many facets of Japanese craft.

The owners of the Asada-ya have a keen interest in ceramics and lacquer ware, which they have collected for generations. Their traditional *kaiseki* meals are often served on this valuable tableware, an indication of the general concern of this *ryokan*.

Above, entryway from the gate to the *genkan* entrance; *below, top,* hors-d'oeuveres in the shape of a table-top landscape; *bottom,* portions of a local *kaiseki* meal; *right,* a guest room showing the garden beyond.

BENI-YA

Over a century ago a local farmer found a hot springs and decided to build a spot. This is how Awara Onsen began, a hot-springs resort that it is called "the living room" of the Osaka-Kyoto Kansai region.

And among the inns that were built there the oldest is the Beni-ya, founded in 1884. Its present owner is the fifth generation of the family which originally ran this fine *ryokan,* known for the *sukiya*-style architecture of its main wooden buildings and for its fine Japanese garden which changes during the season since the flowering plants are so arranged.

Since the inn is equally near the Japan Sea the cuisine is famous for its fish. Particularly well known is the *kaiseki* cuisine of the Beni-ya which features the freshest of sea food.

An indication of the care with which the inn is run is the fact that no guest, during his order stay, is ever served the same meal twice. Careful track is kept as to just who has eaten what and no repeats are tolerated.

This attitude has made the Beni-ya popular among the most discerning of guests. Staying there have members of the imperial family, artists, authors and even people from show-business.

Above, a typical seafood *kaiseki* meal. *Right, top to bottom*: one of the special suites; a view of the garden; the banquet room with a stage for Noh plays; the hot springs bath.

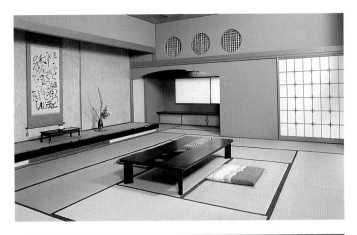

KAIKA-TEI

Another fine *ryokan* at the Awara Onsen hot-springs resort is the Kaika-tei. Established in 1911 it has long enjoyed a most distinguished partongage among the guests having been not only various Prime Ministers but also the Emperor and Empress of Japan.

One of the attractions of this inn is the garden, a very large one, nearly fourteen thousand square meters in size. The garden view form the "Shorai" suite, where the Emperor and other important guests are accomodated, is especially commanding.

The food at the Kaika-tei is another attractions. The style is Kyoto *kaiseki* and especially famous are the Echizen crab and sweet shrimp in winter.

The large bath facing te garden is one of the most restful. It is always brimming with the medicinally excellent hot water of the Awara springs and assures the most relaxed comfort.

Left, top to bottom: the "Shorai" room for important guests; a part of the garden as seen from the lobby; the inn as seen from the garden; the bath. *Right,* portion of a typical *kaiseki* meal.

HIIRAGI-YA

Established in 1818, the Hiiragi-ya in Kyoto has been called one of the finest in the country. Many have thought so and the guestbook includes the names not only of Nobel-Prize laureates Yasunari Kawabata and Hideki Yukawa, but also foreign luminaries as various as Charlie Chaplin and Pierre Cardin.

In striking contrast to the busy Kyoto downtown where it is located, the Hiiragi-ya is a small world of peace and tranquility. *Hiiragi* means "holly," in Japan a sacred tree and one which keeps, it is believed, evil at bay. Here the holly-leaf is a trademark and its form is found on lanterns, plates, trays, etc. Each of the thirty-three guests rooms, all with a view of the traditional garden, bear this distinctive mark.

Evil is kept far away in this quiet and friendly inn. The first thing, indeed, that meets the eye is a framed work of expert calligraphy in the entryway which, translated, says: "The arriving guest feels that he is coming home."

Opposite page: above, gold fan-patterns on *fusuma* doors; *below,* Kyoto *kaiseki.*
Above, a guest room; *below,* the traditional *genkan* entrance; *right,* the bath.

TAIKAN-SO

Located on a hilltop not far from Atami Station the Taikan-so was built originally as a villa in 1940 and was then converted into an inn in 1949. Its name was given it by the celebrated artist, Taikan Yokoyama. He was so impressed by the grand view of mountains, islands and the sea that he have the place his own name which happens to mean a large and grand view.

The eight-acre garden utilizing the slope of the hill, was designed by another famous figure, the landscape architect Matsunosuke Tatsui. Many fine trees were transplanted here, some of them said to be up to three hundred years old.

Over the years a number of additional rooms have been constructed and there are now forty-four in all, varying from the traditional-style to the Western, all of them enjoying a view of the garden.

Top, a view of the garden from a latticed window; *bottom,* the *ryokan* and its gardens.

Top, a *kaiseki* meal; *center,* the corridor connecting guest rooms and main building; *bottom,* a guest room in the *shoin* style.

AWATA-SANSO

Originally built in 1937 as a private villa, the Awata-Sanso was converted into a *ryokan* in 1953. Taking advantage of its location in the foothills of the Higashi-yama mountains of Kyoto, it is placed in a magnificent Japanese garden full of trees and flowers and containing stone lanterns nearly one thousand years old. The building itself is in strict *sukiya* style, one which harmonizes perectly with the garden. One of the qualities of this combination of garden and house is that the view from the second floor is just as fine as that from the first.

The Awata-Sanso is also famous for its food. This is authentic Kyoto cuisine. Seasonal foods, selected from the local markets by the chef himself, are expertly prepared and served on tableware which brings out the beauty of the broiled trout or the grilled eggplant or the slips of bamboo root. And the chef keeps a record of what he has served each guest so that it may be used for reference when the guest next visits.

Left, the entryway. *Right, top,* a view of the buildings; *center,* a guest room with a garden view; *bottom,* a typical *ryokan* meal.

ARAI RYOKAN

Situated in the center of the Izu peninsula in the hot-springs town of Shuzenji, the Arai Ryokan is famous for its garden. Aged trees and large rocks are carefully arranged in this elegant two-acre garden which does indeed resembled a Chinese-style landscape painting.

The building itself extends to the edge of the garden pond and gives one the impression of being afloat in this enchanting landscape. Equally attractive is the famous bath. Based on historical researches it is designed by the celebrated artist, Yukihiko Yasuda, according to the style of the eighth century.

The Arai Ryokan, home to many artists and intellectuals during its long history, is also known for its art collection. The guest rooms themselves are decorated with masterpieces and there is now a plan to build within these walls a real museum to house the rest of the extensive collection.

Top, the facade; *center,* the building and its gardens; *bottom,* a special *kaiseki* lunch; *right,* the *Tempyo-buro* bath.

YAGYU-NO-SHO

A short drive from Shuzenji in the Izu peninsula the Yagyu-no-sho stands, a *sukiya*-style building surrounded by a bamboo forest. Originally a traditional Japanese restaurant in downtown Tokyo it was moved to its present location in 1970.

The reason was that the old neighborhood was becoming too crowded and the cuisine no longer fit its environment. So the entire establishment was moved to an environment that did. Here one may experience authentic Kyoto-style *kaiseki* (tea-ceremony) food as prepared by a chef with fifty years of experience. And here each room contains a small hearth, called a *kiriro,* where every morning the maids prepare fresh *miso* soup for breakfast.

Above, a guest room, *left,* a dedicatory inscription; *right,* the *kendo* hall.

This fourteen-room inn is built around a bamboo garden modeled after that of a famous Nara swordsmen's *dōjō*. The inspiration of Japanese *kendo* fencing is also found in other ways, in the ornaments and decorations of the inn, for example. This expresses the hospitality of the Yagyu-no-sho, an extention of the grave courtesy of the *yagyu* swordsmens' schools.

Above, the bath; *below*, the entrance; *far right*, various kinds of traditional Japanese cuisine.

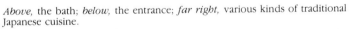

NARA-YA

Founded in 1944, the Nara-ya in the Hakone mountains has a very long history. Fourteen generations of the same family have managed it. It was an officially appointed inn for the feudal lords passing through the Hakone gate, and after the Meiji Restoration both the emperor and empress stayed there.

The inn is located in the heart of the mountains, along a massive slope which holds the twelve-acre garden and, besides the main building, eight annexes are scattered over the garden. These, which vary in size and structure, accomodate from five to twenty guests apiece and one of them is noted for its *goten*-style architecture with its typical high ceilings.

In addition, there are hotsprings baths, one to each room, which are, naturally, operative twenty-four hours a day. In this region the hot water has a reputation for being efficacious against arthiritis.

Below, left, view of the Nara-ya; *right,* typical traditional seasonal cuisine. *Right,* a guest room with a view of the garden and the montains beyond; *opposite page,* the bath, a latticed door, a stone lantern in the garden.

SEKITEI

Sekitei is the name for a small franchise of inns located in both Atami and Izu Nagaoka. They are famous for their rock gardens and for their food.

The gardens are among the most elaborate of their genre. Rocks have been carefully selected and brought to Izu from all over Japan. There, they have been expertly placed to perform their time-honored role of enhancing the natural aspect. This combination of rocks, trees, and water which is the Japanese garden then allows the building of structures which can harmoniously exist in such proximity.

At the Sekitei inns traditions *kaiseki* is served, prepared from local ingredients by experienced cooks. This exquisite cuisine is then appreciated as it ought be—amid the comforts and beauties of nature.

Above, the rock garden; *left,* examples of *kaiseki* cuisine; *below,* the rock walk leading to the annex.

Appendices

List of Ryokan
Glossary Index

List of Ryokan

And, finally, some advice to the guest:

The *ryokan* charge normally includes two meals, dinner and breakfast. If the guest orders lunch as well he will be charged extra.

When making a reservation it is best to do so through a travel agent or some other Japanese-speaking person. There are few *ryokan* that take reservations in English or in languages other than Japanese because the majority of *ryokan* have no English-speaking staff.

The *ryokan* charge is determined by the number of persons using the room, not by room charge itself. Since the price refers to the charge of one person per night, two or three staying in the same room would be charged two or three times the single rate.

Thus, particularly during the tourist season, it is possible that a single guest would not be able to get a reservation since it is just better business for the *ryokan* to prefer a group.

Finally, the *jochu-san* maid is attached to the room and not to the guest. That is, it is her duty to take full care of the occupants of the room from check-in to check-out. She cannot be changed because the room is her duty. The guest may fully count upon her and her services remembering that good mutual relations can make the *ryokan* stay pleasant for both.

A ARAI RYOKAN

970, Shuzenji, Shuzenji-cho, Tagata-gun, Shizuoka-pref.
Rooms : 41
10 minutes from Shuzenji Station by car
Price: 13,000yen—35,000yen

0558-72-2007

ASABA RYOKAN

3450-1, Shuzenji, Shuzenji-cho, Tagata-gun, Shizuoka-pref.
Rooms : 27
6 minutes from Shuzenji Station by car
Price: 13,000yen—30,000yen

0558-72-0700

ASADA-YA

23, Jitsukenmachi, Kanazawa-shi, Ishikawa-pref.
Rooms : 5
5 minutes from Kanazawa Station by car
Price: 33,000yen—50,000yen

0762-31-2228

ASA-YA HACHIBANKAN	813, Taki, Oaza, Fujiwara-machi, Shioya-gun, Tochigi-pref. Rooms : 40 5 minutes from Kinugawa-onsen Station by bus Price: 20,000yen—50,000yen	0288-77-1111
ATAMI SEKITEI	6-17, Wada-cho, Atami-shi, Shizuoka-pref. Rooms : 38 5 minutes from Atami Station by car Price: 22,000yen—26,000yen	0557-83-2841
AWATASANSO	2-15, Sanjobo-cho, Awadaguchi, Higashiyama-ku, Kyoto-shi, Kyoto Rooms : 10 15 minutes from Kyoto Station by car Price: 20,000yen—	075-561-4908
B BENI-YA	4-510, Awara-cho-onsen, Sakai-gun, Fukui-pref. Rooms : 23 6 minutes from Awara-onsen Station by car Price: 15,000yen—20,000yen	0776-77-2333
C CHIKUBA	2-6-22, Yunokawa-cho, Hakodate-shi, Hokkaido Rooms : 37 10 minutes from Hakodate Station by car Price: 7,000yen—15,000yen	0138-57-5171
CHORAKUEN	323, Tamatsukuri, Tamayu-cho, Yatsuka-gun, Shimane-pref. Rooms : 102 7 minutes from Tamatsukuri-onsen Station by bus Price: 10,000yen—25,000yen	08526-2-0111
E ENRAKU	347-1, Unazuki-machi, Shimoniikawa-gun, Toyama-pref. Rooms : 80 3 minutes from Unazuki-onsen Station on foot Price: 10,000yen—35,000yen	0765-62-1211
F FUJIISO	Yamada-onsen, Takayamamura, Kamitakai-gun, Nagano-pref. Rooms : 30 15 minutes from Susaka Station by car Price: 10,000yen—28,000yen	02624-2-2711
FUJI-YA RYOKAN	557 Miyakami, Yugawara-machi, Ashigarashimo-gun, Kanagawa-pref. Rooms : 25 6 minutes from Yugawara Station by car Price: 12,000yen—20,000yen	0465-62-3711
FUKUICHI RYOKAN	Kohachi, Ikaho-machi, Kitagumma-gun, Gumma-pref. Rooms : 56 17 minutes from Shibukawa Station by car Price: 12,000yen—40,000yen	0279-72-3113
FUNA-YA	1-33, Yunomachi, Dogo, Matsuyama-shi, Ehime-pref. Rooms : 43 10 minutes from Matsuyama Station by car Price: 15,000yen—20,000yen	0899-47-0278
FUTAMIKAN	569-1, E, Futami-cho, Watarai-gun, Mie-pref. Rooms : 29 (Main & Annex), 14 (New Building) 15 minutes from Ujiyamada Station by car Price: 12,000yen—32,000yen	05964-3-2003
G GAJOEN	1-8-1, Shimomeguro, Meguro-ku, Tokyo Rooms : 35 3 minutes from Meguro Station on foot Price: 10,000yen—15,000yen	03-491-4111

| GENMYOAN | 32, Monju, Aza, Miyazu-shi, Kyoto
Rooms : 32
10 minutes from Amano-hashidate Station on foot
Price: 10,000yen—30,000yen | 07722-2-2171 |

| GIMBASO | 25, Oyama, Nishiura-cho, Gamagori-shi, Aichi-pref.
Rooms : 101
28 minutes from Gamagori Station by bus
Price: 10,000yen—30,000yen | 0533-57-3101 |

| GORA KANSUIRO | 1300, Gora, Hakone-machi, Ashigarashimo-gun, Kanagawa-pref.
Rooms : 15
3 minutes from Gora Station on foot
Price: 20,000yen—23,000yen | 0460-2-3141 |

H HANARE GYOKUTEI — 501, Yumoto, Hakone-machi, Ashigarashimo-gun, Kanagawa-pref.
Rooms : 8
4 minutes from Hakone-yumoto Station by car
Price: 20,000yen—37,000yen — 0460-5-7501

| HAPPOEN | 12-1, Minaguchi-cho, Atami-shi, Shizuoka-pref.
Rooms : 20
6 minutes from Atami Station by car
Price: 10,000yen—20,000yen | 0557-81-6125 |

| HASHINO-YA BEKKAN RANSUI | 1684 Arima-cho, Kita-ku, Kobe-shi, Hyogo-pref.
Rooms : 10
30 minutes from Shinkobe Station by car
Price: 25,000yen—35,000yen | 078-904-0651 |

| HIIRAGI-YA RYOKAN | Main Building : Oike-kado, Fuya-chodori, Nakagyo-ku,
Kyoto-shi, Kyoto
Annex : Nijo-sagaru, Gokomachi-dori, Nakagyo-ku,
Kyoto-shi, Kyoto
Rooms : 33 (Main Building), 14 (Annex)
15 minutes from Kyoto Station by car
Price: 20,000yen—60,000yen | 075-221-1136 |

| HORAI | 750-6, Izusan, Atami-shi, Shizuoka-pref.
Rooms : 17
5 minutes from Atami Station by car
Price: 20,000yen—55,000yen | 0557-80-5151 |

| HOSEIKAN | 1191-1, Tamatsukuri, Tamayu-cho, Yatsuka-gun, Shimane-pref.
Rooms : 50
10 minutes from Tamatsukuri-onsen Station by bus
Price: 7,000yen—35,000yen | 08526-2-0011 |

| HOTEL BANKOKU-YA | 1, Tei, Yuatsumi, Atsumi-machi, Nishitagawa-gun, Yamagata-pref.
Rooms : 88
5 minutes from Atsumi-onsen Station by car
Price: 8,000yen—22,000yen | 0235-43-3333 |

| HOTEL EBINA | 5-12, Nagisa-cho, Ito-shi, Shizuoka-pref.
Rooms : 57
3 minutes from Ito Station by car
Price: 10,000yen—30,000yen | 0557-37-3111 |

| HOTEL HYAKUMANGOKU | 11-2-1, Yamashiro-onsen, Kaga-shi, Ishikawa-pref.
Rooms : 155
10 minutes from Kaga-onsen Station by car
Price: 15,000yen—25,000yen | 07617-7-1111 |

HOTEL SHOWAEN	3178, Minami-taeishi, Beppu-shi, Oita-pref. Rooms : 33 5 minutes from Beppu Station by car Price: 10,000yen—35,000yen	0977-22-3211
HOTEL SUIMEIKAN	1268, Koden, Gero-cho, Mashita-gun, Gifu-pref. Rooms : 183 3 minutes from Gero Station on foot Price: 10,000yen—60,000yen	05762-5-2800
I ICHIRIKI RYOKAN	4-161, Atami, Atami-machi, Koriyama-shi, Fukushima-pref. Rooms : 42 4 minutes from Bandai-atami Station on foot Price: 8,000yen—35,000yen	0249-84-2115
ISHIKARISANSO	337-1, Tonoharu, Chikushino-shi, Fukuoka-pref. Rooms : 21 5 minutes from Futsukaichi Station by car Price: 7,000yen—16,000yen	092-922-3961
IWASO	375, Miyajima-cho, Saeki-gun, Hiroshima-pref. Rooms : 8 (Main Building), 5 (Annex), 32 (New Building) 15 minutes from Miyajima-sanbashi on foot Price: 14,000yen—40,000yen	08294-4-2233
IZANRO IWASAKI	365, Misasa, Misasa-cho, Tohaku-gun, Tottori-pref. Rooms : 104 25 minutes from Kurayoshi Station by bus Price: 10,000yen—35,000yen	0858-43-0111
IZUNAGAOKA SEKITEI	55, Minamionoue, Nagaoka, Izunagaoka-cho, Tagata-gun, Shizuoka-pref. Rooms : 22 5 minutes from Izunagaoka Station by car Price: 22,000yen—26,000yen	05594-7-2841
K KAIKATEI	Awara-cho-onsen, Sakai-gun, Fukui-pref. Rooms : 37 10 minutes from Awara-onsen Station by car Price: 15,000yen—30,000yen	0776-77-2525
KAGA-YA	Kochi 73-1, yobu, Wakura-machi, Nanao-shi, Ishikawa-pref. Rooms : 180 5 minutes from Wakura Station by bus Price: 15,000yen—20,000yen	0767-62-2111
KAJIKAEN	55, Okutsu, Okutsu-cho, Tomata-gun, Okayama-pref. Rooms : 31 10 minutes from Okutsu-onsen Station on foot Price: 13,000yen—30,000yen	08685-2-0121
KAJIKASO WARAKUTEI	17-62, Nishiyama-cho, Atami-shi, Shizuoka-pref. Rooms : 10 10 minutes from Atami Station by car Price: 23,000yen—40,000yen	0557-81-5223
KAMATA	784, Miyakami, Yugawara-machi, Ashigarashimo-gun, Kanagawa-pref. Rooms : 15 10 minutes from Yugawara Station by bus Price: 20,000yen—30,000yen	0465-62-2151
KAMOGAWA GRAND HOTEL	820, Hiroba, Kamogawa-shi, Chiba-pref. Rooms : 136 3 minutes from Awakamogawa Station by car Price: 19,000yen—30,000yen	04709-2-2111

KANAGU-YA HOTEL	2202, Hirao, Oaza, Yamanouchi-machi, Shimotakai-gun, Nagano-pref. Rooms : 29 5 minutes from Yudanaka Station by car Price: 10,000yen—20,000yen	02693-3-3131
KASHOEN	1-15, Yumoto, Hanamaki-shi, Iwate-pref. Rooms : 40 15 minutes from Hanamaki Station by car Price: 10,000yen—30,000yen	0198-27-2111
KASUGA HOTEL	40, Noborioji-cho, Nara-shi, Nara -pref. Rooms : 44 3 minutes from Nara Station on foot Price: 11,000yen—25,000yen	0742-22-4031
KATSURAGI KITANOMARU	2505-2, Ugari, Fukuroi-shi, Shizuoka-pref. Rooms : 29 45 minutes from Hamamatsu Station by car Price 16,500yen—	05384-8-6111
KAYOTEI	1-Ka-2, Higashi-machi, Yamanaka-machi, Inuma-gun, Ishikawa-pref. Rooms : 10 15 minutes from Kaga-onsen Station by car Price: 20,000yen—	07617-8-1410
KIKUSUIRO	1130, Takabatake-cho, Nara-shi, Nara-pref. Rooms : 17 3 minutes from Nara Station by car Price: 20,000yen—	0742-23-2001
KIKU-YA RYOKAN	874-1, Shuzenji, Shuzenji-cho, Tagata-gun, Shizuoka-pref. Rooms : 54 5 minutes from Shuzenji Station by car Price: 9,000yen—20,000yen	0558-72-2000
KINEYA SAZANTEI	2861, Omachi-onsenkyo, Omachi-shi, Nagano-pref. Rooms : 29 15 minutes from Shinano-omachi Station by bus Price: 13,000yen—35,000yen	0261-22-4411
KINJOKAN	10-33, Showa-cho, Atami-shi, Shizuoka-pref. Rooms : 114 7 minutes from Atami Station by car Price: 18,000yen—35,000yen	0557-81-6261
KINUGAWA KANA-YA HOTEL	1394, Ohara, Fujiwara-machi, Shioya-gun, Tochigi-pref. Rooms : 50 3 minutes from Kinugawa-onsen Station on foot Price: 25,000yen—50,000yen	0288-77-3600
KINZAN	1302-4, Arima-cho, Kita-ku, Kobe-shi, Hyogo-pref. Rooms : 29 20 minutes from Shinkobe Station by car Price: 13,000yen—28,000yen	078-904-0701
KIUNKAKU	4-2, Showa-cho, Atami-shi, Shizuoka-pref. Rooms : 35 5 minutes from Atami Station by car Price: 20,000yen—35,000yen	0557-81-3623
KIYOMIZU RYOKAN	588, Yumoto-takidori, Hakone-machi, Ashigarashimo-gun, Kanagawa-pref. Rooms : 10 10 minutes from Odawara Station by car Price: 30,000yen—	0460-5-5385

KOCHIKADAN	3964-1, Itsuku, Kochi-shi, Kochi-pref. Rooms : 18 5 minutes from Kochi Station by car Price: 10,000yen—30,000yen	0888-45-2100
KOSHINOYU	1108, Yukawa, Oaza, Nachi-katsuura-cho, Higashimuro-gun, Wakayama-pref. Rooms : 82 3 minutes from Kii-katsuura Station by car Price: 10,000yen—20,000yen	07355-2-1414
M MATSUDA-YA HOTEL	3-6-7, Yuda-onsen, Yamaguchi-shi, Yamaguchi-pref. Rooms : 40 15 minutes from Ogori Station by car Price: 13,000yen—30,000yen	0839-22-0125
MIYAZAKI RYOKAN	320, Unzen, Obama-cho, Minami-takaki-gun, Nagasaki-pref. Rooms : 111 1 hour & 30 minutes from Isahaya Station by bus Price: 9,000yen—40,000yen	095773-3331
MOMIJI-YA	Takao-cho, Umegahata, Ukyo-ku, Kyoto-shi, Kyoto Rooms : 17 (Main Building), 12 (Annex) 30 minutes from Kyoto Station by car Price: 13,000yen—30,000yen	075-871-1005
MONJUSO BEKKAN	Monjudo-misaki, Amano-hashidate, Miyazu-shi, Kyoto Rooms : 14 3 minutes from Amanohashidate Station on foot Price: 8,000yen—25,000yen	07722-2-2151
MURAO RYOKAN	1-28, Shinyu, Kaminoyama-shi, Yamagata-pref. Rooms : 95 2 minutes from Kaminoyama Station by car Price: 7,000yen—35,000yen	02367-2-2111
N NAGOYA	1-1-18, Sakuragaoka, Ito-shi, Shizuoka-pref. Rooms : 14 1 minutes from Minami-ito Station on foot Price: 15,000yen—25,000yen	0557-37-4316
NANZANSO	1056, Nagaoka, Izunagaoka-cho, Tagata-gun, Shizuoka-pref. Rooms : 37 5 minutes from Izunagaoka Station by car Price: 8,000yen—50,000yen	05594-8-0601
NARA-YA RYOKAN	162, Miyanoshita, Hakone-machi, Ashigarashimo-gun, Kanagawa-pref. Rooms : 12 (Main Building), 8 (Annex) 5 minutes from Miyanoshita Station on foot Price: 20,000yen—35,000yen	0460-2-2411
NISHIMURA-YA	469, Yushima, Kinosaki-cho, Kinosaki-gun, Hyogo-pref. Rooms : 42 5 minutes from Kinosaki Station by car Price: 20,000yen—30,000yen	079632-2211
NISHIYAMA BEKKAN	678-1, Sanba-cho, Onomichi-shi, Hiroshima-pref. Rooms : 9 (Main Building), 6 (Annex) 10 minutes from Onomichi Station by car Price: 15,000yen—33,000yen	0848-37-3145
NUNOHAN	3-2-9, Kogandori, Suwa-shi, Nagano-pref. Rooms : 44 2 minutes from Kamisuwa Station by car Price: 12,000yen—30,000yen	02665-2-5500

O OCHIAIRO	1887-1, Amagi-yugashima-cho, Tagata-gun, Shizuoka-pref. Rooms : 62 25 minutes from Shuzenji Station by bus Price: 12,000yen—28,000yen	05588-5-0014
OHITO HOTEL	1178, Yoshida, Ohito-cho, Tagata-gun, Shizuoka-pref. Rooms : 120 (Main Building), 9 (Annex) 3 minutes from Ohito Station by car Price: 9,500yen—55,000yen	0558-76-1771
OSAKA-YA	356, Kusatsu, Oaza, Kusatsu-machi, Gumma-pref. Agatsuma-gun, Rooms : 36 5 minutes from Kusatsu-onsen Station on foot Price: 15,000yen—30,000yen	027988-2411
OTANISANSO	2208, Hiramachi, Aza, Fukawa-yumoto, Nagato-shi, Yamaguchi-pref. Rooms : 105 3 minutes from Nagato-yumoto Station by car Price: 10,000yen—30,000yen	08372-5-3221
R RYOKAN SHIKITEI	1163, Takabatake-cho, Nara-shi, Nara-pref. Rooms : 18 3 minutes from Nara Station by car Price: 18,000yen—30,000yen	0742-22-5531
RYOKAN TSURUGATA	1-3-15, Chuo, Kurashiki-shi, Okayama-pref. Rooms : 13 10 minutes from Kurashiki Station on foot Price: 9,000yen—27,000yen	0864-24-1635
RYUGUDEN	139, Motohakone, Hakone-machi, Ashigarashimo-gun, Kanagawa-pref. Rooms : 20 40 minutes from Odawara Station by car Price: 18,000yen—40,000yen	0460-3-7111
RYUSEKI	1012, Yoshida, Ito-shi, Shizuoka-pref. Rooms : 38 15 minutes from Ito Station by car Price: 23,000yen—40,000yen	0557-45-2266
S SAGASAWAKAN	400-1, Kadonohara, Amagi yugashima-cho, Tagata-gun, Shizuoka-pref. Rooms : 34 15 minutes from Shuzenji Station by car Price: 12,000yen—21,600yen	05588-5-0115
SAIKI BEKKAN	70, Yamada, Oaza, Misasa-cho, Tohaku-gun,Tottori-pref. Rooms : 52 25 minutes from Kurayoshi Station by bus Price: 15,000yen—35,000yen	08584-3-0331
SANYOSO	270, Mamanoue, Izunagaoka-cho, Tagata-gun, Shizuoka-pref. Rooms : 20 3 minutes from Izunagaoka Station by car Price: 38,000yen—45,000yen	05594-8-0123
SASA-YA HOTEL	3055, Togura, Oaza, Togura-machi, Hanishina-gun, Nagano-pref. Rooms : 73 5 minutes from Togura Station by car Price: 10,000yen—50,000yen	02627-5-0338

SEIKORO	3-467, Gojo-sagaru, Toiyamachi-dori, Higashiyama-ku, Kyoto-shi, Kyoto Rooms : 25 7 minutes from Kyoto Station by car Price: 13,000yen—30,000yen	075-561-0771
SEIRYUSO	2-2, Kochi, Shimoda-shi, Shizuoka-pref. Rooms : 34 5 minutes from Izukyu-shimoda Station by car Price: 15,000yen—30,000yen	05582-2-1361
SEKIYOTEI	1300, Gora, Hakone-machi, Ashigarashimo-gun, Kanagawa-pref. Rooms : 36 5 minutes from Gora Station on foot Price: 10,000yen—25,000yen	0460-2-2461
SHIGETOMISO	31-7, Shimizu-cho, Kagoshima-shi, Kagoshima-pref. Rooms : 20 6 minutes from Kagoshima Station by car Price: 12,000yen—30,000yen	0992-47-3155
SHINMATSUNOE	3-21-29, Ifuku-cho, Okayama-shi, Okayama-pref. Rooms : 53 5 minutes from Okayama Station by car Price: 10,000yen—30,000yen	0862-25-5131
SHIROGANE-YA	18-47, Yamashiro-onsen, Kaga-shi, Ishikawa-pref. Rooms : 16 10 minutes from Kaga-onsen Station by car Price: 13,000yen—30,000yen	07617-7-0025
SHUSUIEN	5-27-27, Yunohama, Ibusuki-shi, Kagoshima-pref. Rooms : 47 5 minutes from Ibusuki Station by car Price: 10,000yen—50,000yen	09932-3-4141
SUMI-YA RYOKAN	Sanjo-sagaru, Fuya-cho, Nakagyo-ku, Kyoto-shi, Kyoto Rooms : 26 15 minutes from Kyoto Station by car Price: 15,000yen—40,000yen	075-221-2188
SUWASO	7, Rokasu-machi, Nagasaki-shi, Nagasaki-pref. Rooms : 12 5 minutes from Nagasaki Station by car Price: 13,000yen—30,000yen	0958-22-1877
TACHIBANA-YA RYOKAN	3, Tei, Yuatsumi, Atsumi-machi, Nishitagawa-gun, Yamagata-pref. Rooms : 68 5 minutes from Atsumi-onsen Station by car Price: 7,500yen—25,000yen	0235-43-2211
TAIKANSO	7-1, Hayashigaoka-cho, Atami-shi, Shizuoka-pref. Rooms : 43 3 minutes from Atami Station by car Price: 25,000yen—43,000yen	0557-81-8137
TAKINO-YA	162, Noboribetsu-onsen-cho, Noboribetsu-shi, Hokkaido Rooms : 72 15 minutes from Noboribetsu Station by bus Price: 8,000yen—50,000yen	01438-4-2222
TAMANOU RYOKAN	2731-1, Kawakami, Oaza, Yufuin-cho, Oita-gun, Oita-pref. Rooms : 10 35 minutes from Beppu Station by car Price: 13,000yen—25,000yen	0977-84-2158

TAWARA-YA RYOKAN	Anenokoji-agaru, Fuyacho-dori, Nakagyo-ku, Kyoto-shi, Kyoto Rooms : 19 15 minutes from Kyoto Station by car Price: 20,000yen—50,000yen	075-211-5566
TENSEIEN	682, Yumoto, Hakone-machi, Ashigarashimo-gun, Kanagawa-pref. Rooms : 48 15 minutes from Yumoto Station on foot Price: 15,000yen—17,500yen	0460-5-5521
TOKIWA HOTEL	2-5-21, Yumura, Kobu-shi, Yamanashi-pref. Rooms : 47 (Main Building), 10 (Annex) 10 minutes from Kofu Station by car Price: 10,000yen—30,000yen	0552-52-1301
TOKOEN	2155, Kaike, Yonago-shi, Tottori-pref. Rooms : 90 15 minutes from Yonago Station by car Price: 10,000yen—20,000yen	0859-34-1111
TORIKYO	824, Izusan, Atami-shi, Shizuoka-pref. Rooms : 33 5 minutes from Atami Station by car Price: 18,000yen—35,000yen	0557-80-2211
TSUBAKI	Okuyugawara, Yugawara-machi, Ashigarashimo-gun, Kanagawa-pref. Rooms : 24 10 minutes from Yugawara Station by bus Price: 20,000yen—60,000yen	0465-63-3333
W WAKAMATSU	1-2-27, Yunokawa-cho, Hakodate-shi, Hokkaido Rooms : 22 10 minutes from Hakodate Station by car Price: 13,000yen—35,000yen	0138-59-2171
Y YADA-YA	1-1, se, Katayamazu-onsen, Kaga-shi, Ishikawa-pref. Rooms : 93 10 minutes from Kaga-onsen Station by car Price: 13,000yen—35,000yen	07617-4-1181
YAGYUNOSHO	1116-6, Shuzenji, Shuzenji-cho, Tagata-gun, Shizuoka-pref. Rooms : 14 5 minutes from Shuzenji Station by car Price: 20,000yen—35,000yen	0558-72-4126
YAMADA-YA	1-5-26, Shishito, Ito-shi, Shizuoka-pref. Rooms : 7 2 minutes from Ito Station on foot Price: 18,000yen—26,000yen	0557-37-3312
YONEWAKASO	2-4-1, Hirono, Ito-shi, Shizuoka-pref. Rooms : 18 15 minutes from Ito Station by car Price: 15,000yen—23,000yen	0557-37-5111
YOSHIDASANSO	59-1, Shimooji-cho, Yoshida, Sakyo-ku, Kyoto-shi, Kyoto Rooms : 11 20 minutes from Kyoto Station by car Price: 30,000yen—50,000yen	075-771-6125
YUNOSHIMAKAN	645, Yunoshima, Gero-cho, Mashita-gun, Gifu-pref. Rooms : 46 5 minutes from Gero Station by car Price: 10,000yen—30,000yen	05762-5-3131

Glossary Index

amado   Lit. rain-door, a sliding shutter which closes the open verandas of the traditional Japanese house during bad weather, when the occupants are away, or at night. *15*

andon   A paper-paned lamp-stand which can be used in the room or the garden; though originally designed for candles, most now contain electric bulbs. *25*

ayu   A Japanese freshwater fish which resembles and is often confused with trout; *ayu* is eaten fried, salt broiled or as *ayu-zushi*—fresh *ayu* with vinegared rice. *30*

banto   Originally a clerk or a secretary, the term *banto* is now almost entirely applied to the *ryokan* man whose duties are those of the bell-captain, head porter or concierge in western hotels. *10*

bento   A lunch box; it can vary from the plainest and simplest variety to a grand array of lacquer boxes filled with delicacies; all, however, are designed with the season and the specialities of the region in mind. *35*

Buddhism   See: Zen Buddhism.

byobu   Standing screen—comes in various sizes, single or in pairs, each of which may have up to six leaves; beautifully decorated, often works of art, these screens typify Japanese aesthetics. *13*

Byodo-in   An 11th-century temple compound near Uji, southeast of Kyoto, its so-called Phoenix Hall is the finest example of existing Heian period architecture. *46*

cha-no-yu   Lit. "tea hot-water," this is the so-called "tea ceremony" of Japan, a ritualized partaking of tea, often with a meal *(kaiseki),* and always a full cognizance of the place, the occasion, the season, and those within whose company one joins this quiet, beautiful occasion. *9, 19*

choshi   A saké bottle. *31*

chozubachi   Lit. a washing-water basin, i.e. a hand-basin; now almost always used to refer to the stone basins in the gardens outside tea-ceremony houses—here the guests rinse their hands before entering. *21*

75

dojo	A practice hall or area, a term only used in connection with Japanese sports such as *kendo* fencing, Judo, and Karate. *61*
Edo	A term—lit. "river-mouth door"—which refers to the former name of Tokyo, the capital of Japan—and to the period in Japanese history (1600-1868) when Edo culture predominated. *11*
engawa	A veranda, structurally a space which serves as transition from inside to outside in Japanese architecture, as seen in the materials from which it is made—unfinished wood, a material considered midway between the soft *tatami* mats of the interior and the hard stone garden outside. *23*
fusuma	A kind of sliding door—the other kind is the *shoji* door (a framework covered with translucent paper)—made of pressed papers and light woods. *15*
futon	Japanese bedding, padded mattresses and quilts pliable enough to be folded and stored. The *futon* mattress is the *shiki-buton* and the cover is the *kake-buton*. *5, 15, 31, 38*
genkan	The vestibule of the Japanese house, a raised area one mounts to enter the house, and where one often sits to remove shoes before entering; structurally, the *genkan* serves as an intermediate area between outside and inside. *9, 13, 51*
geta	Outdoor footwear, a wooden platform with two crosswise supports, the foot fitting into a v-shaped thong on the top. *20, 38*
goten style	An architectural description rather than the name of any precise style. It means palace-style or in the style of an imperial residence.
Gyogi	Or Gyoki, a monk (668-749) remembered as an ascetic with great charisma. Many temples are attributed to him. *11*
hibachi	A charcoal burner used as a source of heat. It comes in various shapes and sizes, is filled with ash, and pieces of charcoal are arranged in the center. The *hibachi* known in the West—a charcoal grill for cooking—is quite different.
hisashi	A term usually now used to indicate the long low eaves of the traditional house, though it can also mean a canopy or a pented roof. *23*
ikebana	The term for Japanese flower arrangement, an art which, as the derivation of the name indicates—from *ikeru* (to keep alive) and *hana* (flowers)—is quite different from Western flora art. The aim of *ikebana* is specifically to bring out the living naturalness of the flowers. To this end, an enormous body of literature exists, from the 7th century to the present day, and there are many schools and disciplines. All, however, agree that it is the hand of man which reveals the natural beauty of the materials. *9, 18-19*
itamae	The proper Japanese word for a cook. *10*

izutsu	A well-curb, i.e. the stone facings and ledge of an open well. *45*
jochu	An term for maidservant. *10, 51*
Kabuki	One of the major three forms of Japanese classical drama, the other two being the Noh and the Bunraku puppet drama. The Kabuki was originally, like the doll drama and unlike the aristocratic Noh, a popular theater and it still retains much of the spectacle and sentiment which endeared it to its original audience. *9*
kaiseki	The meal served at the *cha-no-yu* "tea ceremony." Traditionally it was a light repast, the term coming from the heated stones (*seki*) which early monks placed in the garments (*kai*) next to their stomachs in order to stave off hunger pains. Shortly, however, the food became both refined and expensive, though the portions remained—as they still do—small. Modern *kaiseki* is probably the most elegant form of Japanese cuisine. *30-31, 33, 45, 47, 51, 52-53, 55, 57, 60, 64.*
kare-sansui	Lit. "dry mountain stream," i.e. a waterless rock and sand garden said to have been created from Zen Buddhist precepts but also owing a great deal to the Chinese ink paintings just then (the 14th century) becoming known. In any event, the idea of a symbolic expression of a whole universe within a limited space is common to both. *27*
Kawabata Yasunari	One of the finest of modern Japanese novelists (1899-1972) and the only Japanese to be awarded the Nobel Prize in literature. *54*
kendo	Lit. "the way of the sword," i.e. the art of fencing based on the techniques of the two-handed sword of the samurai. Though originally used for actual combat, it is now a sport with no practical application. *60-61*
kiriro	A small portable hearth used almost exclusively for heating foods. *60*
kimono	See: *tanzen, yukata*
Kyogen	A form of comic drama which evolved along with the Noh and is now most often seen as interludes between the more sober dramas in the Noh theater. There are a number of Noh, however, which incorporate the Kyogen into their structure, and there are now many all-Kyogen performances at the Noh theaters. *9*
matcha	A powdered form of green tea used mainly in the *cha-no-yu* "tea ceremony." *19, 30*
mikan	The Japanese mandarin orange, a loose-skinned variety of tangerine *30*
miso	Been paste—the basis of much Japanese food including *misoshiru* soup, and the many *miso*-dressed varieties of vegetables and fish. *35, 60*
monzen-machi	Lit. "town in front of the gate," or temple-town; a descriptive term often used in opposition to castle-town *joka-machi. 11*

Noh	The major form of Japanese drama as well as the oldest extant professional theater, dating from the 14th century. An aristocratic entertainment, the Noh evolved into a stately drama the protagonist of which is often masked and the Buddhist-influenced plots of which are always historical. The result is often of a transcendental beauty. *9*
nori	Dried, edible seaweed, eaten in combination with other foods or—dipped into soy sauce—by itself. *35*
nuru-en	An open veranda, attached to the room itself. *20*
ocha	Japanese tea: it comes in a number of varieties but is always "green" and hence to be differentiated from the "black" teas of India and the rest of Asia. The finest variety is *gyokuro* which is made of the finest and most tender leaves. *5, 19*
ofuro	The Japanese bath: it comes in many varieties. At the *ryokan* it is usually quite large; in the home it is ofen a tub deep enough for the bather to immerse the body up to the neck. No matter the tub, the etiquette remains the same. The bather washes before entering the tub, then relaxes in the hot water, and leaves it for the next bather to enjoy. *5, 36, 37*
okami	The mistress of *ryokan* or Japanese-style restaurant, often acting as manager and hostess as well. *10, 13, 51*
okayu	A gruel or porridge made of rice, often a part of the traditional Japanese breakfast. *35*
onsen	A spa, a hot springs, many of which are found in volcanic Japan. Though the hot springs are put to many uses in Japan (heating, cooking), they are used mainly for bathing and there are many *onsen-machi* or hot-spring resorts in the country, and many *onsen ryokan*. *11, 36*
ranma	The door transom in traditional Japanese architecture—often open and carved or otherwise decorated. *15, 25*
rotemburo	An outdoor hot-springs pool. *37*
ryori-ryokan	A *ryokan* known for (or where the emphasis is upon) its *ryori*, i.e., its cuisine. *11*
saké	The alcoholic beverage brewed from fermented rice which is to Japan as wine is to Europe. Coming in various grades of varying flavors, saké is not a strong drink—it has the alcohol content of, say, sherry. *5, 31*
sakura	The famed "cherry-blossom" of Japan; actually the tree is deciduous, of the family Rosaceae and no relation to the cherry. The blossom (there is no fruit) is widely admired and has been throughout Japanese history. The early falling petals have come to symbolize for generations the transcience of all things. *28*

sashimi	Fresh fish—tuna, sea bream, etc.—sliced and served with soy sauce and the piquant *wasabi* horse-radish. One of the favorite foods of Japan. *31*
Sen-no Rikyu	Early tea master (1522-1591) who, under the successful general Toyotomi Hideyoshi, became general aesthetic advisor to the whole country. *28*
shakkei	A gardening concept where an available view—a distant mountain, for example, is incorporated into the design for one's own garden. For this reason the term is often translated as "borrowed scenery." *27*
shoin style	Or, *shoin-zukuri,* a style of Japanese residential architecture used in mansions of the military and laity from the 16th through the middle 19th centuries. This style, which formed the basis of the traditional Japanese house, developed from the classical architectural style, the *shindenzukuri. 46, 57*
shoji	A form of Japanese sliding door in the shape of a lattice over which transluscent paper has been pasted. The lambent light which *shoji* creates within the room has been rightly much admired. *14-15, 25*
shun	A Japanese aesthetic often applied to food. Here it connotes the flavor of the seasons—locally bought, naturally prepared seasonal food. *10*
suimono	A clear Japanese soup, somewhat like a consomme. It is always served tepid, usually during the meal, *35*
sukiya style	Or *sukiya-zukuri,* a style of residential architecture which rose in the 16th century. The *sukiya* refers to the building in which the tea ceremony is held and this style combines a rustic simplicity with a sophisticated elegance, exhibiting a most delicate sensibility as seen in the use of natural elements and the elimination of ornamentation. *42, 44, 48, 52, 58, 60*
tabi	A kind of stocking or sock, worn with Japanese clothing. It separates the big toe from the others so that the foot can fit the *geta* thongs of the traditional footwear. *38*
Tanizaki Junichiro	One of Japanese finest modern novelists (1886-1965) and one of the few (Kawabata was another) who understood and respected traditional Japan. *25*
tanzen	A usually thick and sometimes padded long coat worn over the *yukata* kimono. In cooler seasons, it is always offered to guests at the *ryokan* for their strolls in the garden or outside. *38*
tatami	The mat used as flooring in the traditional Japanese room. The size is standardized and so it is common to speak of rooms as being six or eight mat rooms. In Kyoto (there are regional differences) the standard *tatami* mat is 5.3 × 3.1 feet (1.91 × 0.95 meters). *5, 9, 15, 31, 38*
tea ceremony	See: *cha-no-yu*

tempyo-buro	I.e. a bath in the style of buildings in the Tempyo Era (8th century Japan)—thus a reconstructed bath in this supposed style. *59*
tokonoma	The "alcove" built into the main room of the traditional Japanese house. It is a built-in unit raise from the floor and is used for hanging scrolls and placing *ikebana* flower arrangements. In its latter capacity it is often referred to as a means of bringing the outside into the house. *9, 15, 18-19*
tofu	Bean-curd, a food which began in China, was refined in Japan and is now know all over the world. High in nutrition, it is also one of the most inexpensive of all protein foods. *31, 35*
tsuboniwa	One of the variety of small gardens which make use of the odd-shaped bits of land surrounded by the house—a *tsubo* is a unit of space (two *tatami* mats, 35.6ft^2.) and its use indicates the smallness of the garden. *27, 41*
tsukubai	A wash basin in the garden, used in conjunction with the tea ritual—see also, *chozubachi*. *28*
umeboshi	Salt-cured Japanese "plums," thought to aid digestion and stimulate appetite. A favorite in *bento* lunch boxes and at the Japanese breakfast. *35*
Yagyu	Both a district, near the ancient city of Nara, and a now-famous name, that of Yagyu Munenori (1571-1646), the master swordsman who founded the Yagyu or Shinkage school of swordsmanship.
Yasuda Yukihiko	Japanese-style painter (1884-1978) well known for his elegant treatement of Japanese historical themes, for his portraits and for his bird-and-flower paintings.
Yokoyama Taikan	Prominent Japanese painter (1868-1958) known as one of those who developed a new style of Japanese painting that was respectful to past aesthetic traditions. *56*
yukata	A light cotton kimono often used during the summer months and also offered the guest at the Japanese *ryokan* for use within the establishment or for strolls in the gardens or the outside streets. *5, 11, 37-38*
Yukawa Hideki	Theoretical physicist who became the first Japanese—in 1949—to win the Nobel Prize. *54*
zabuton	The large square cushions upon which one sits in the *tatami*-matted Japanese room. *5, 15*
Zen Buddhism	One of the Buddhist sects most influential in Japan. Its aesthetic is seen in the painting, the gardens, the tea "ceremony," in the temple cuisine, the architecture, etc. It is also a discipline, the aim of which is spiritual enlightenment. In this, it is a philosophy as much as it is a religion. *13*